Navigating This Thing Called Life

Navigating This Thing Called Life

MYISHA ALLEN

Text- Lee Johnson

Design- Terry Lewis Photography

Copywright © Myisha Allen

First print June 2020

ISBN 978-1-7352078-1-0

CONTENTS

DEDICATION

would like to dedicate this book to my parents, Malinda and Clifford, who have been with me every step of my journey. My mom is very kind, strong and selfless. My dad has always been the most important man in my life. He has always supported me and made sure I had the best education possible.

I also dedicate this book to my daughters, Miranda and Mylee, who I hope are enjoying navigating our journey together. It can be a struggle being a child of someone who is visually and physically disabled, so I thank you both for your patience. Through this book you will learn my story, and always know that it could not be complete without you two. You inspire me to keep accelerating.

My hope is that people living with disabilities, their parents, and individuals going through difficult times can find inspiration in my story.

My life has been a long, difficult, unexpected journey; however, with all its curves and roadblocks, I have still managed to navigate this thing called life.

1

MISTAKES TO MIRACLES

For the first forty-five minutes of my life, I was stuck between two worlds. I was a perfectly healthy baby, trapped in the world of my mother's womb trying to navigate my life to the world outside. Waiting on the outside for me were my teenage parents. My mother was very petite, so she was instructed not to have a vaginal delivery. She selected the doctor that was supposed to perform her C-section, but my mom unexpectedly went into labor early, while he was on vacation and I was delivered by another doctor vaginally.

My parents were excited because according to the ultrasound and my growth during the pregnancy, they were expecting a perfect baby girl. Forty-five minutes-I was stuck in the womb. Forty-five minutes- I was trying to navigate to the outside world. Forty-five minutes was enough for this doctor, so he decided to pull me out with forceps. Unfortunately in doing so, I was faced with my first road block.

tell us to get anything we wanted. I can remember sweeping my head from left to right-side to side- chips, cookies, ice cream, sodas, gum—which would I choose? I'll take them all! I felt like Weezie from the Jefferson's because on Friday's I would always move on up.

Vivid visual moments like that are really precious to me. I had no idea how much they would truly mean until later on in life. I had a modest childhood, but they always made sure I had good Christmases, birthdays, and new clothes. We would also go to Virginia Beach and Busch Gardens yearly. My mom was the sleepover queen, making our sleepovers the envy of the neighborhood. My grandparents doted on me as their first grandchild. I could do no wrong in their eyes. While being the apple of my grandparents' eyes, my mom started to notice a change in my eyes. I was walking into objects and squinting frequently. Although I had some visual impairment at birth, my vision was declining even further and the color was changing. Upon visiting the doctor, I was diagnosed with cataracts. Cataracts at five years old- how rare! The cataracts were removed at age seven and I had to wear thick bifocals in order to see.

As if that wasn't enough, here comes another roadblock, I was simultaneously diagnosed with Juvenile Rheumatoid Arthritis. The inflammation from my arthritis would build up on my corneas which caused uveitis, a white or grey clouding. This made navigating life harder because now everything in my view was foggy. I would go in every two years so they could scrape my corneas to remove the cloudy inflammation. At times, I felt like a meteorologist because the excruciating pain from the inflammation would increase with rain or a change in weather. While I could feel pain in my eyes, I couldn't feel pain in my right arm because of the paralysis, which put me in harm's way many times. I have a lot of scarring on my arm to prove it.

Growing up in a home without central air, we had uncovered radiators. As a young child, I would place my right arm on a radiator and not feel it getting burned. I also burned my arm on an iron and didn't feel it. These mishaps required trips to the hospital and one of the doctors called the state to report my burns. I almost got removed from my mom's home.

As an adult, I now know how hard it is to watch your kids 24/7. When I burned myself as a child, it wasn't my mom's fault, because I still burn myself to this day. I also had a problem of biting on my right arm because I couldn't feel it. Whenever I would cry, get frustrated or upset, I would bite my arm. Therefore, my family would wrap it in socks and bandages to prevent me from further hurting myself.

Once I almost lost my whole finger. I put a mini rubber band on my finger and forgot that it was on there. I couldn't feel that I was losing sensation. Later while playing, I noticed that my finger was the size of a sausage. My aunt Nicole rushed me to the doctor and they thought it would need to be amputated. Thankfully they took me to the Children's

Hospital of Philadelphia (CHOP) where they were actually able to save my finger. This is an example of one of my miracles.

Although I was very accident prone, my family never treated me differently. They expected the same from me as my other siblings.

When they taught my siblings how to tie their shoes, they taught me as well. When they got a bike, I got a bike. If they had to do the dishes, I had to do the dishes. Having chores made me very independent.

Despite all of my miraculous accomplishments, I was teased horribly at school. They would call me Steve Urkel, Four Eyes and One Arm. I can laugh now, but I was definitely crying then. The kids were so cruel that I would come home and cry to my grandparents. I would literally try different methods every week to break my glasses. In my heart, I wanted to be able to navigate without glasses, but the reality was I desperately needed them; however, I was willing to sacrifice my vision so the teasing could cease. I recall one day in third grade when a boy took my glasses and threw them across the schoolyard. My glasses were shattered. A part of me was happy that someone succeeded in breaking my glasses, but now I couldn't see. I came home and told Pop Pop- he was not going for that. He strolled up to that school like George Jefferson and said in front of the entire class, "The next person who teases her is going to have to deal with me." Fear of man didn't last long in the hearts of those kids. They were back to being cruel in no time. They called me Teacher's Pet, as they threw fingers in my face, because I had to sit in the front of the class in order to see the board. I ate lunch and had recess by myself because I had no friends. The miraculous thing is despite the loneliness and bullying; I found a way to focus on my work and achieved straight A's.

Sometimes in life you are thrown a much needed lifeline, an alternate route. My lifeline was given to me in third grade by being sent to Overbrook Educational Center, which is a public school that has classes for visually impaired students. When I attended, it had a mainstream side and a visually impaired side. The kids were definitely a lot nicer because they were already used to going to school with blind children. It was such a different atmosphere that I quickly made friends. I went from being a zero to a hero. For once, would you believe I was now popular? I excelled in academics and track and field. Not only was I a hero at school, but in 1994, people say that I became a hero for my family. There was a bad fire at our home. My mom buckled under pressure, so she was running around screaming at the top of her lungs and trying to put out the fire. Meanwhile, all of my siblings were in shock and just froze in place. I did everything they taught and prepared me for at Overbrook. Despite my cataracts, juvenile arthritis, and use of one arm, I was able to save all four of my siblings and my mother at the age of nine years old. It was devastating because the fire happened a week before Christmas and we lost everything.

2

BACK TO EARTH

I n 1995 my hero, my protector, was involved in a car crash that took his life. The same car that made me feel like I was sitting on top of the world by pulling up to the Wawa and getting anything I wanted, is the very same car that crashed my world and took the life of my Pop Pop. How can the thought of one vehicle bring the highest of highs and the lowest of lows?

My family thought that it was a good idea to bring in an older male family member to provide protection for us. We would have never thought that we would need protection from the protector! We didn't know we were inviting evil into our home. Not only was the evil in our home, but he crept into my bed. He sexually abused me from the ages of thirteen to fifteen. My brother actually turned out to be my protector because he caught him in the act one night. When my parents found out I had been violated, they immediately pressed charges and he got arrested. Unlike other families who don't believe the accusations of their children, my parents acted so fast that he was arrested the next day. This entire ordeal messed up my mental and moral compass so much that my younger siblings slept with me in order to protect and calibrate me.

Unfortunately, some family members turned their backs on me and my Mom Mom. I was so devastated because I couldn't understand how they could blame or be mad at me when I was an innocent victim. I was just a child and this caused me to have a lot of unnecessary guilt. I was thinking that it was my fault for the family disunity, but how could it be if I was just telling the truth? If I had stayed silent, would my family still be together?

After the family member was arrested, the state removed me from my mother's home. They decided that my new permanent destination was now living with my dad. Don't get me wrong, I love my dad, but again, I was the innocent victim and I am the one being punished. I was removed from my home, my mom, my sisters, my brothers, my Mom Mom. On top of all of this, some of my extended family turned their backs on me. They accused me of lying and making everything up. Why would I lie about something so evil? Why are the adults who are supposed to support and protect me the ones hurting me?

When we went to trial, some of these family members harassed us at the courthouse. The tension was so thick, that a fight broke out between one of them and my mom in the courtroom. Low and behold, my mom got arrested. How is she getting arrested for protecting me? In my mind, things couldn't get any worse.

Although I was mandated through the state to seek counseling as part of the Special Victims' Program, I didn't take it seriously. I was going through the motions, fulfilling the requirements. I didn't take the prescribed anti-anxiety medicine. I didn't complete any stupid assignments. As soon as the trial was over, I discontinued therapy. I convinced my mom that I was ok and didn't need it. This was probably the worst decision ever. I didn't want therapy, but I really needed it. I guess I just wasn't mentally ready to accept it. But honestly, I appeared strong to everyone on the outside, but inside, I was hurting so bad. All of the obstacles and roadblocks were taking their toll on me- being visually impaired with cataracts and bifocals, only having the use of one arm, being teased as a child, the sexual abuse, the trial, the family drama, and being ripped from my home. It was just too much for a fifteen year old. At this point, I wanted to stop navigating all together. I wanted to be at the end of the road. If life had a power button, I wanted to push it and turn completely off. In order to stop my pain, I took a lot of capsules of acetaminophen. I was young, so I didn't realize you couldn't overdose on acetaminophen. It might not kill you, but it can give you the worst stomach ache ever. My throat was sore for days. That was my first attempt at suicide and I am ever so grateful that I didn't

of health conditions I would soon have to manage. Prior to 2008, the only disabilities that were known to me were my visual impairment and the paralysis of my right arm. Who knew that bringing another life in this world would jeopardize mine?

I spent eleven out of thirty-two weeks of my pregnancy in the hospital. When they would treat one thing, another issue would appear. I tried to manage things on my own because my mom was diagnosed with breast cancer the year before, so I didn't want to burden her with my issues. She was still receiving chemo during my pregnancy. I didn't want to tell my dad either, because remember, I think I am grown. Therefore, I was trying to navigate this pregnancy thing on my own.

Deven and I, together, had to figure out this thing called life. I had to deliver my daughter, Miranda, at thirty-two weeks because I had really bad preeclampsia. I also developed a medical condition called hyperemesis gravidarum, which causes excessive vomiting, that kept me in the hospital often. The constant vomiting put a strain on my already delicate and impaired eyes and I was now diagnosed with a partial retinal detachment. This caused me to lose even more vision.

At the hospital, they put a line in my arm to give me proper nutrients and I developed a blood clot in my arm. At this time, they discovered that I have a blood clotting disorder. I was also diagnosed with Grave's Disease.

However, the scariest health complication I experienced during this time was during labor itself. I'm trying to be strong and navigate Miranda's heart beats from inside my womb into this world and unbelievably- I go into cardiac arrest! That's how they learned that I also had Peripartum Cardiomyopathy (PPCM), which is a rare, uncommon form of heart failure that happens during the last month of pregnancy. I also developed sinus tachycardia which is a rapid irregular heartbeat.

Miranda's delivery was also full of surprises. After being in the hospital for two weeks, I was released on February 12th. They said that I would return to be induced on February 22nd. However, the next morning, I had the most excruciating headache and acid reflux ever. The heartburn was a feeling I had never felt before. I also kept vomiting, so I was miserable. Deven wanted to take me right back to the hospital. I had just got released after two weeks so I didn't want to make a U-turn right back to the hospital. I assumed it was normal pregnancy symptoms, just elevated since I was advancing closer to my delivery date. Deven didn't agree, but I convinced him that I would be ok, so he went to work at 1 p.m. At 6 p.m. I couldn't lift my head off the pillow. I had vomited so much that I was choking and it was coming from my nose. My ears were ringing. My chest was burning. I was so sick that when Deven came home at 9 p.m., he found me on the floor curled up in a ball. Deven immediately rushed me to the emergency room. My mom met us at the hospital. Although the doctors induced me that night, they said that since it was my first pregnancy, I probably wouldn't deliver Miranda for another twenty-four hours. The doctors stabilized my headache and the acid reflux with some meds and now I was feeling wonderful. I sent my mom home and Deven on to work. I told my mom I would call her when I went into labor and Deven was coming back later. When Deven returned he sat with me for a couple of hours but the doctors said delivery would still be a while, so he went home to get a shower.

I fell asleep but was abruptly awakened by ringing bells, flashing lights, beeping machines and white coats surrounding me. They were calling so many codes that I was immediately alarmed. What's going on? "We need your mom now!" I was crying and nervous because I didn't know what was going on. My mom was working twenty-five minutes away. Deven was working twenty-five minutes away. The doctors said that Miranda had to come out of me right then. I suddenly realized that I was going to have to navigate this delivery on my own. The doctors then rushed to prep me for surgery. Wait! I was planning to have her vaginally. "We need to get this baby out!" The medical team wheeled me quickly into the surgical room and as soon as they were about to open me up, Deven busted into the room. "You have two minutes to scrub up!"

After delivering Miranda by C-section, she went right to neonatal intensive care and I went right to the ICU.

I didn't know until the next day that the reason they rushed me to the ICU was because I went into cardiac arrest. That's when I was diagnosed with PPCM. The bad heartburn that I experienced wasn't acid reflux, it was my heart enlarging and restricting my oxygen. I literally could have died!

Miranda was born on February 14, 2008 weighing 3 lbs. and 6 oz. She was my little miracle. My heart swelled at the sight of her. Since this pregnancy had damaged my heart, I was told I should never get pregnant again.

Having Miranda made me mature a lot. I was now a parent and had someone else I had to guide through life. However, my long list of medical issues was a big part of my life now too. I spent most of my twenties trying to navigate being a family of three and having tons of doctor appointments. When I say I had appointments, I had to see the endocrinologist, the cardiologist, the pulmonologist, the hematologist, the retina specialist, the cornea specialist and the rheumatologist. I wasn't the only one with medical issues. Miranda had asthma and acid reflux so she was in and out of the hospital frequently as well. Thankfully, Deven was there to take care of us both.

I was still able to get around, but not independently. I could see Miranda and people's faces, but I never went anywhere by myself. This decline in my vision caused me to visit a cornea specialist in 2008. All the years of scraping my lens, so I wouldn't have cloudy vision, caused scar tissue to develop. My new cornea specialist suggested a cornea transplant. I immediately declined. I was young and didn't care about things that were not completely broken. I was used to my broken eyes.

At the age of twenty-four I decided to let my eighteen year old little brother, Kenny move in with me. I was taking care of myself and my medical issues, my daughter and her medical issues, and now Kenny and his medical issues. He moved in with me because my mom was battling breast cancer and none of my other siblings lived on their own. Kenny and I were very close because we shared a special bond. We were the only siblings with disabilities, so we understood each other. Kenny had hydrocephalus, which is a buildup of fluid in the brain that causes brain damage. He had seizures and was developmentally disabled. I felt it was my duty as his big sister to protect him. I had disabilities, so I knew what was needed to take care of someone with them. He needed help navigating this thing called life and I was going to help him do it.

In 2010, I noticed that my emotions were like a roller coaster and I was diagnosed with bipolar disorder. My primary care doctor kept urging me to see a therapist on a regular basis, but with all that I had going on, I had a hard time prioritizing my mental health. If I had an appointment with the therapist and the cardiologist, in my mind, I needed to check on my heart instead of my head. Little did I know the damage of not taking care of my mental health would cause. I found myself praying more because this was a scary time in my life.

4

ROLLERCOASTER

As I think back to those summer trips to Clementon Park and Busch Gardens, I always loved roller coasters. With all the things that were simultaneously going on in my life, I felt like I was in the front seat of one. I was thrilled about my future, but so scared of it at the same time. I was excited to be a new mom, but in doing so, I walked away with a bad heart and a ton of new medical issues. The doctors told me explicitly not to have another child. I always wanted more than one child. I knew the joy that siblings bring. I grew up with multiple siblings on both sides of my family. It was my sibling that saved and protected me from further sexual abuse. I was now the sibling that was being a protector and taking care of Kenny. The thought of not providing Miranda with a sibling spiraled me beyond postpartum depression. My bipolar depression was kicked into high gear, as if it took the seat next to me on the roller coaster.

Louise; the Laverne to my Shirley. That was the first of many adventures we would embark upon.

Julia and I went on a cruise to the Bahamas and she somehow convinced me to do Karaoke. My cousin decided to join us on stage and we cleverly gave ourselves the name, "Three Blind Mice". Can you imagine us on stage, not knowing the words, not being able to see the words, and me and Julia looking everywhere but in the right direction? It took the crowd a moment to realize that we were in fact blind. However, once we were done, they gave us the biggest standing ovation. I still laugh when I think about it.

Another time, Julia had the bright idea of taking our daughters ice skating in NYC. After walking up to the counter and requesting our shoe size, we asked if we could have a personal assistant because we were visually impaired. My mom said the look of confusion plastered on the lady's face was priceless. She informed her manager of our request and he was even more shocked. They told us to just hold on to the railing and skate around slowly. Our blades were cutting the ice at one mile per hour, but we were ice skating! That is until Julia grabbed on the wrong thing and fell right out of the rink. Everyone came rushing to assist her, but she was fine. We laughed about it for the rest of the trip. My mom was so proud of us that she called everyone she knew to tell them we had the courage to ice skate.

People are always amazed when Julia and I do things that most blind people won't attempt. In addition to going to the movies, we swim, and have gone on four cruises. Once, while on a cruise in Mexico, we signed up for jet skiing. "Who's going to ride who?" he asked. That would literally be the blind leading the blind. He finally understood that we needed someone to ride with us and we received our ride for free.

The experiences with Julia taught me that I don't have to hide anymore. I make it known I'm visually impaired and ask for the help I need. Julia taught me what she knew all along, that even with disabilities, life goes on.

6

IN THE DARK

I n 2012, I was finally convinced to get the cornea transplant. It was a dual surgery, a team effort between a cornea specialist and a retina specialist. The retina specialist went first and did my left eye, the strong eye. After he repaired the retina, the cornea specialist went in and transplanted the cornea. I would go every day to get my eyes and sutures cleaned. The first two days after surgery, my vision was horrible. I could only see shapes. On the third day, when the patch was removed, it was like the heavens opened up. I saw clearer than I ever saw in my life. I was absolutely amazed. I thought people looked one way, but now they looked completely different. Wait a minute! All this time I had a mole under my eye? Are you serious?! I was no longer looking through a cloud. BEST!!!-DAY!!!-EVER!!! Since the surgeries were nine hours long, and it was risky to be under anesthesia within a short period of time, we decided to wait on doing the transplant in my right eye. I wasn't complaining because I was surely ready to navigate my life with the clearest vision I had ever known.

In the beginning of 2014, I was scheduled for the transplant on my right eye. I had the same retina specialist, but there was now a new cornea specialist. I felt a little uncomfortable because I like to get to know you before I let you in my personal space. But the reality was that I needed to get it done. The surgery was a success and I was feeling amazing. Six months later, one of the sutures in my right eye got infected. That caused the new cornea to reject itself. This had a domino effect, causing the left eye to reject itself as well. Why was this happening? Should I have just left the right eye alone? Surprisingly, I wasn't as depressed as I could have been. I was just thankful for the amount of time that I was given to see the world clearly, especially seeing Miranda.

In 2016, I started feeling tingles in my left arm and my phone kept falling out of my left hand. My whole left side became numb, and I would just fall because my left leg couldn't support me. The doctors did an MRI and said that my Chiari malformation was acting up. I was confused and asked what that was. They were surprised that I didn't know about it because it was in my medical records all along. There is no way of managing it, because it usually doesn't cause any problems. But you know my life, so of course it caused me problems. I was immediately sent to a neurosurgeon who said that if we don't operate, there will be irreversible damage and I would never regain the feeling in my left arm. That's my good arm.

The thought of not having use of my left arm terrified me. Growing up, I always told myself that I would never get surgery on my brain or my heart. For the Chiari Malformation surgery, they remove a piece of your skull to lessen the pressure. The pressure has nowhere to go so the blood vessel bends in a way that it shouldn't. They remove a piece of your skull to give the vessel room to expand. I informed the neurosurgeon that I was not interested in having the procedure. I will get back to you if I change my mind. Well, I had to change my mind sooner than I thought.

A week later, my caregiver and I are at a convenience store and I trip and fall in the aisle. I fell down on my left side and it aggravated my Chiari Malformation. I was in so much pain that it was decided that I needed to have the surgery immediately or risk losing the feeling in my left arm. My good arm. Although it terrified me to have another surgery, especially on my brain, not having the use of my left arm terrified me even more. However, I was not prepared for what would happen next. I woke up from the surgery with no vision. My fear going into surgery was that I wasn't going to wake up at all. I didn't fear losing the rest of my vision. That was the furthest thing from my mind. I went on another emotional roller coaster. I was mad at myself because I went against my gut feeling of not wanting the surgery.

The doctors told me to give it time. They said that once I healed, my vision, as I knew it, would come back.

While in the hospital they kept me in a dark room to prevent the light from bothering my eyes or causing migraine headaches. After being discharged, it continued to be dark for days. One day my mom said that it was nice and sunny outside. I told her to open the blinds so that I could see and feel the sun shining on my face. The blinds were open! I told her to cut the lights on so I could see. The lights were on! I thought I was in the dark for recovery purposes. I had no idea that my recovery was darkness. I was on heavy pain meds so my mom thought I was just having side effects and talking crazy from the meds. We were both surprised to know that my vision was not coming back. After a couple of days, I regained depth perception. I could see shapes, but that was it. I can't see faces. I can't see color. The doctors insisted that this has never happened before. Of course it hasn't happened to others, but freak accidents always happen to me! Why me?

The irony of it all is that I had just started working for the National Suicide Prevention Lifeline. Here I was trying to do something good, to save people from their dark, hopeless tunnel vision and now I lose mine. How is this fair? How am I going to navigate taking care of myself, my daughter and my brother without any vision? I started to question my faith. Why would God let me go through all of this?

Emotional roller coaster, here I come again. However, I finished the ride and worked for the National Suicide Prevention Lifeline for two years helping others and myself.

7

RAISING MY M&MS

Miranda was young, but she was already used to helping me navigate, so to her, my loss of sight didn't change things. However, our lives were changing in other ways. In 2018, I was experiencing severe back pain. I assumed it was caused by another blood clot. Deven took me to the emergency room and after they ran all the blood tests the doctor said, "We have good news and bad news." The good news was I didn't have a blood clot. The bad news was they couldn't give me a CAT scan because I was pregnant.

"No I'm not." "Yes, you are." "Maybe you guys got my urine mixed up with somebody else's? I'm not pregnant."

Blood tests don't lie. I was pregnant. Given my complicated medical history, I called all my doctors and together they put a plan in place. I was put on a blood thinner to prevent blood clots. I had to be vigilant with my blood pressure medicine to keep my blood pressure under control. I was placed on a baby aspirin regimen to preserve the function of my heart. I also had to visit the endocrinologist to make sure my thyroid levels were stabilized. My team followed my pregnancy very closely.

The plan was to carry for thirty-nine weeks. The doctors said it was safe for me to have a vaginal delivery, but I opted for another C-section. I thought it would be safer for me and my child. At thirty weeks, I went in for my bimonthly ultrasound and the baby wasn't growing like it should. The doctors told me they would continue to closely monitor me and to return the next week. When I returned at 31 weeks and 3 days, the baby still wasn't growing like it should. After checking my blood pressure, they decided I wasn't going home this time. I had preeclampsia again. I had to stay in the hospital for three more weeks.

After a couple of days the doctors said they were not picking up a lot of movement on the ultrasound. The new plan was to induce my pregnancy the very same day. My second little miracle, Mylee, came at exactly thirty-two weeks on January 31, 2019.

Amazingly my heart corrected itself by twenty percent during my pregnancy with Mylee. The mortality rate after cardiomyopathy is very high. I'm blessed that my case didn't need a heart transplant, like my younger cousin. Although Mylee's delivery was a breeze compared to Miranda's, caring for her was not. Shortly after having her, my life completely turned upside down.

I was back in line for another ride on the emotional

roller coaster. It was one of the happiest and saddest of times of my life. Happy, because I had a new baby that I adored. However, exactly sixty days from having Mylee, my little brother, Kenny passed away. Now I was extremely sad. I'm going through all of this and would you believe Deven had the nerve to leave us completely. I also decided to move from my home because it was just too hard for me to be there. Walking by Kenny's room was too much to bear. Kenny was like the son I never had, so his death felt like losing a child. This brought back the raw feelings of losing my Mom Mom to cancer in 2005. I felt like I lost a mother and a son, but I still have my mother and I never had a son.

I was angry at Deven. He knew all that I was going through. He was close to Kenny. He took care of all of us. How could he just up and leave me? I was feeling so many emotions at the same time that I felt like all of the seven dwarfs in one body. Then my mind started playing tricks on me again. The thought of pushing that power button was starting to enter my mind. But this time, I prayed a lot and my children kept me sane. I knew I needed to be here for them. I felt guilt and sorrow, but Mylee gave me the hope and love that I needed. My emotions kept going back and forth. I felt guilty for being happy and guilty for being sad. It took me a while to stabilize my mind and honestly, I still struggle with these feelings to this day. I know from working the National Suicide Prevention Lifeline, that first, you have to identify that the person is truly suicidal. Second, you have to determine if they have a plan and then you have to find out what is important to them. You have to find that thing that will give them a glimmer of hope; something to live for. I had to treat myself like a caller. I was living for my children and my mom. I needed to be here to take care of my children. Deven left them. How could I leave them too? My mom is still feeling the pain of losing a child. I couldn't have her lose another one. My children and my mother kept me navigating. I also knew that Kenny wouldn't want me to be so depressed because he was always so happy. I am so proud of myself for continuing to push through. I now put much more focus on being a great mother. Mylee is growing so fast. She is starting to recognize colors and shapes. She has somehow learned that my eyes don't look like her eyes, and tries to pull them out for a closer look. I can't see her little fingers, so I am getting poked in the eye constantly, which is dangerous for me. I might have to get an eye patch before she completely destroys my eyeballs.

Mylee likes to hide from me. I will call her name and she can be right in front of me and will be silent. When I walk away, she will laugh and run to me. It's amazing what children can figure out at such a young age. I am grateful for all of the experiences that I had with Miranda when I had my vision. I will do those things with Mylee, but it won't be the same experience for me. Deven and I took Miranda to Disney World for Christmas when she was six years old. For her 8th birthday, she had a sleepover and then we all went to the American Girl store in NYC. After lunch, we went ice skating at Rockefeller Center. For her 9th birthday; the two of us took a cruise to the Bahamas. This past summer, we took a road trip with my mom and cousins to my sister's house in GA. My mom returned home, and another cousin picked us all up and we drove to her house in SC. I had to take the Amtrak train home by myself with all the kids. This experience was different because in the past, I had Julia to accompany me and I had some vision. This time, I had no Julia and no vision. Mylee was also just seven months old. But guess what? I did it! I am so proud of myself. These adventures are difficult for me, but I know Miranda appreciates my efforts.

One of the things that I treasure most in life is that I know what Miranda looks like. I remember her pretty smile, long and skinny legs, light brown skin, glasses (but not bifocals like me), hair braided with a bunch of barrettes, brown eyes and dirty brown hair. We also have the same mole under our eyes. Did I mention her smile? She is my twin.

On the other hand, what I regret most in life is I have no idea what Mylee looks like. I can't give you descriptive details. I have to rely on other people to tell me how she looks. Imagine having to rely on the subjective thoughts of others telling you how your own child looks. They can never see her how I would see her. I'm her mother. I should be able to describe her to you.

Sometimes in life you get to a point where you have to yield. I notice that I am most yielding when it comes to Miranda. Miranda is now twelve and starting to give me attitude. She's at that age where kids are trying to find themselves and where they belong. Let's not forget that her dad left, her uncle died and now she has to share my time and attention with a sibling. She was an only child for eleven years. Kenny was Miranda's best friend. Although he was twenty six when he died, developmentally he was twelve; Miranda's age. They were inseparable. I recognize how difficult 2019 was for her and sometimes I feel bad for all that she has lost at a young age. I feel bad that she is the child of someone physically disabled. Unfortunately, I have to rely on my child to help me move around in the world. People say I spoil her, but you have to understand that I am limited in what I can do for her. I can't help her with her homework. I can't drive her to the mall. I can't pick out her outfits. I can't walk her to school. I admit it. I'm more yielding with her because I feel guilty. I'm more yielding with her because it's something I CAN do. Do you realize that I have to borrow her eyes on a daily basis? I need her eyes to read the mail. I need her eyes to give me credit card numbers to pay bills. I need her eyes to help me navigate life. Her eyes are constantly looking out for me, when I should be looking out for her. Miranda also helps out with Mylee. However, since my mom is in remission, she has truly stepped up to help me take care of my girls.

After Kenny died and Deven left, my mom quit her job in corporate America to help me take care of myself and the children; especially, Mylee. I need assistance taking care of her. When I had Miranda, I had some vision and didn't need much help. Surprisingly, it's not hard for me to change Mylee's diaper. Most people are amazed that I can do it with no sight and one arm. My mom thinks I am too paranoid and overprotective, but I have a strong fear of something happening to my baby. One day, my fear turned into reality. When Mylee was six weeks old, my mom was dressing her and she started turning blue.

My mom said, "She's not breathing." I said, "What do you mean she's not breathing?!" I started screaming. This was my fear coming true. I didn't know what to do. I called 911 and they gave us instructions to clear her airway and she started breathing again. What haunts me the most is that while she was choking and trying to catch her breath, she didn't make a sound. Imagine if I was alone with her. I would have thought she was sleeping and I could have lost my baby. I have reasons to be paranoid.

Looking back at raising Miranda and Mylee, my M&Ms as my dad calls them, I have more patience at 34 than I did at 22. I'm wiser and I don't get as frustrated easily. I think I am navigating motherhood much better now, especially with having the support of my mom and dad.

Although I have my disabilities, I enjoy everything about being a mom. If you are disabled and are contemplating having a child, I say go for it. Raising children is hard, whether you are disabled or not. There is no right way to navigate the job of parenting. Just surround them with love, keep them safe and enjoy the ride.

8

LOVE IS BLIND

had been with Deven since I was nineteen. Basically, all of my adult life. Our families grew up together in the same neighborhood. Since he knew me and my issues, there wasn't much explaining to do. That made dating him so much easier. I didn't know, until we broke up, how hard it would be dating with a disability.

Don't get me wrong, I have dated since he left, it just hasn't resulted in anything serious. Disabled or not, the fun part of a relationship is the beginning. After that, things can get complicated. While I've had fun dating, I get tired of the silly questions: How do you text if you can't see? How did you have a baby? How do you (insert task) if you are blind?"

Surprisingly, I don't get offended because if you don't know, you don't know. But I do get tired of the questions.

Recently, against my better judgment, I went with my sisters to a nightclub. I hate nightclubs. They give me anxiety. It's too dark and the music is too loud. When you're blind, you rely heavily on your hearing and your hearing is extremely heightened. I can be in one room and hear someone turn on the light switch in another room. I can actually hear the energy change in the room. You might not know this, but everything gives off sound and vibrations. Therefore, being in a loud place is overwhelming and makes me feel like I am suffocating. As a result, the nightclub is the last place I want to be.

The cornea transplants made my eyes sensitive to light, therefore, I always wear sunglasses. I admit that sometimes I like that they hide my eyes, so people can't immediately tell I'm blind. At the nightclub, a cute guy (at least in my sister's opinion) approached me and we began talking. The conversation was good enough that we exchanged numbers. Our phone conversations were intriguing, so we decided to have a first date. When I explained the logistics of how he would need to walk with me, he was confused. He didn't realize I was visually impaired. He just thought I was being cool in the club rocking my shades. I was nervous that he would cancel the date, but he didn't. However, the question game started.

"How did you text me?' "How did you call me?" I answered them and he didn't seem to be bothered, so we saw each other every other day for two weeks straight. At the same time, I was in the process of filming YouTube videos about my life and my sister posted one on her Instagram feed and he viewed it. Although he knew I was visually impaired, he didn't know I only had the use of one arm.

He asked why I didn't tell him. I'm thinking to myself, you're not the one that is blind, we hung out so many times, how could you not know? He stopped talking to me and my heart was broken. He tried to make up excuses, but I knew the real reason.

I'm now trying online dating and am presented with another dilemma. Do I come out and tell them from the beginning that I'm blind? However, if I come out and say it, could I be making myself a target of a dishonest person? When am I supposed to tell them? Do I wait until I get to know them? If I do that, will they feel like I was being dishonest? I'm still trying to figure out how to navigate this dating thing. I must say that I do prefer online dating. I don't have the usual hang ups that people have with it. For most people, the first thing that attracts them to someone is physical appearance. I can't see them, so that's not important to me. I'm baffled when my friends continue to date a guy they think is cute, but complain that he is a jerk. For me, I would just be dating a jerk, not a cute jerk!

I also visualize people by their voice. In my world, your voice is my attraction. I listen to tones and inflections to determine your personality. If a guy doesn't have a great voice, I am not attracted to him. Overall, I just go with my gut feeling. If he sounds like a cocky, arrogant person, nine times out of ten, he won't accept my disabilities. I just use my personal judgment and assess each situation individually.

Whether you have a disability or not, dating is hard. I'm going to be thirty-five this year and I hope marriage is in my future. Since I'm not getting any younger, it makes me wonder if I have to lower my standards because of my disabilities. However, I know my worth. I know I deserve a good man and will find him one day. I won't settle, because I don't settle.

Even though it's difficult, I'm still going to have hope and navigate this dating game. People say love is blind as a cliché, but for me, at least physically, it really is!

9

TAKING CARE OF ME

When I look back at all I have been through, I thank God I am still here to share my story. Whenever I visit a new doctor, they are amazed at my medical history. I assure them that I am 34 and not 80. One even said I should write a medical book. Well here it is-it's not medical, but it's my book!

One thing I have learned in my journey is that self-care is really important. I attended therapy sporadically throughout my life, but I never took it seriously until the age of 30. I went twice a week and never missed an appointment because I actually loved it. That's when I was diagnosed with Bipolar Disorder. I was prescribed talk therapy sessions and medication. Mentally, this was the best I ever felt. Knowing that my goal is to be a motivational speaker, my therapist linked me with public speaking training courses. I even won a Toastmaster public speaking certificate.

I have severe mood changes daily due to my bipolar disorder. It makes me feel like I never got out of the front seat of that roller coaster. What hurts the most is that people don't take mental health seriously because they can't see it. I have been accused of crying wolf about it. It's not me crying wolf. It's actually you crying wolf for me. In turn, when I have an episode and need help, you won't be there, because you don't believe me. It's my shoulder everyone leans on when they need emotional support. But when I need support- I'm looking for shoulders. Now I am stressed, which brings on an anxiety attack. Breathe; take a deep breath; get back to self-care.

Self-care includes doing things that you enjoy. Everyone's joy is different. Fancy linen tablecloths, crystal wine glasses, a delectable four course meal against the backdrop of your favorite band playing could be considered the perfect evening for you. It's a recipe for severe anxiety served on a silver platter for me. I tend to focus on ten things at one time and give them all equal amounts of attention. Therefore, my anxiety is overloaded in crowded places. I can hear chefs in the kitchen cooking, toasted glasses clinking, soft whispers of soon to be lovers at the bar, and forks ever so lightly grazing plates. All of the sounds are equally close and equally clear. It can be so overwhelming that it hurts. This now leads to an anxiety attack. I must now employ one of my self-care regimens in order to relax.

Audio books are therapeutic for me. They let me escape the present and navigate to the future. I just put on my headphones and get lost in the world of my book. I love all genres. I have my favorites, where I recite all the words as its being read to me. Once complete, I do mental book reports and identify key facts. This monopolizes my thoughts and allows me to get lost in my head.

Nature sounds soothe my soul as well. I fall asleep to the sound of steady rain. Oftentimes, when I awake and it isn't really raining outside, I like to bend my neck in a shampoo bowl and get my hair done. A spontaneous trip to the nail salon is nice as well; especially since I only pay half price. That's right- the one arm special!

My sense of humor prevents me from being miserable. I refuse to let my disabilities make me bitter. Without sight, I still try to see as much of the world as possible. Parasailing, jet skiing and swimming with dolphins have all been crossed off my bucket list. There is so much left for me to see and do in this world. Not having sight gives me the freedom to envision things exactly how I hope them to be.

The most important lesson is to take care of you first. Helping people is very important. It's at the core of who I am. However, you can't give someone else CPR if you are dead. Save yourself first. Always remember that you are not better than anybody else, but nobody else is better than you. Believe in yourself. Achieve your dreams. Don't make excuses of why you can't- find the reasons why you can. Know your triggers. Know your strengths. Know your sorrows. Know your joys. Know you. Know that you can successfully overcome anything life puts on your path.

In my life I have had many medical mistakes and miracles. Attending Overbrook School for the Blind allowed me to soar in NASA's Space Camp, but the sexual abuse gave me a crash landing back to earth. When I found my heart, it was literally and figuratively broken, spiraling me on an emotional roller coaster, but with therapy, I know that life goes on. Raising my M&M's in the dark, is challenging as a single parent. I can attest that, like me, love is blind, but I never give up hope in finding it again. Until then, I am taking care of me.

As I reflect on the year of 2020, with all of its obstacles, although I may not have 20/20 vision, I am still navigating this thing called life.

GET IN TOUCH WITH ME

 Navigating_thisthingcalledlife

 myishaallen@mindysentertainmentgroups.com

Made in the USA
Middletown, DE
25 February 2021

34293574R00035